My BASEBALL Season

A journal of my skills,
my games, and my memories.

Karleen Tauszik

TIP
TOP
BOOKS

Published by Tip Top Books, Dunedin, Florida

Summary: This journal provides children with a place to track their baseball season: their games, practices, areas of improvement and contribution, and their fun memories.

ISBN-13: 978-1985623743
ISBN-10: 1985623749

Karleen Tauszik is the author of books for children ages 8-12. Visit her on the web at KarleenT.com, where you can see her other books and sign up for her newsletter.

This book belongs to

_____

My Baseball Season

from _____ to _____
        Date   Date

Hurrah! You're on the team!

This journal is the perfect place to track your baseball season—your practice sessions, your games, the highlights of the season, and all the fun you'll have.

Here's what you'll find inside:

First, there are four pages to journal your pre-season weeks of practice.

Next, there are enough pages to journal up to 30 games, so you have enough for preseason games, the main season, and a few for tournaments. Need more? One is reserved for photocopying.

In between each game page, you'll find a page to journal how your practice sessions are going.

At the end, there are seven blank pages to fill with photos, extra notes, statistics, and mementos. You can even get all your teammates to write notes and their autographs if you like. Add whatever you want to so you remember your baseball season and make this book uniquely yours.

Good luck and have a great season!

Pre-Season Practice

The week starting _____

Coach's focus this week is: _____

_____

_____

My focus this week is: _____

_____

_____

How I feel starting out: _____

_____

_____

What I think I can contribute to the team this week: _____

_____

_____

My notes about this week's practice: _____

_____

_____

_____

_____

_____

_____

_____

_____

Pre-Season Practice

The week starting _____

Day & Date

Coach's focus this week is: _____

_____

_____

My focus this week is: _____

_____

_____

How I feel starting out: _____

_____

_____

What I think I can contribute to the team this week: _____

_____

_____

My notes about this week's practice: _____

_____

_____

_____

_____

_____

_____

_____

Pre-Season Practice

The week starting _____
Day & Date

Coach's focus this week is: _____

_____

_____

My focus this week is: _____

_____

_____

How I feel starting out: _____

_____

_____

What I think I can contribute to the team this week: _____

_____

_____

My notes about this week's practice: _____

_____

_____

_____

_____

_____

_____

_____

_____

Pre-Season Practice

The week starting _____

Day & Date

Coach's focus this week is: _____

_____

_____

My focus this week is: _____

_____

_____

How I feel starting out: _____

_____

_____

What I think I can contribute to the team this week: _____

_____

_____

My notes about this week's practice: _____

_____

_____

_____

_____

_____

_____

_____

_____

Game Day

Game Date: _____   Game Time: _____

We played against: _____   Home ☐   Away ☐

Positions I played: _____ Final Score: _____

My summary: _____

_____

_____

_____

Coach's comments: _____

_____

_____

My contributions: _____

_____

_____

_____

Where I could have done better: _____

_____

_____

_____

Highlights of the game: _____

_____

_____

_____

_____

Practice

Starting _____ until our next game on _____
Day & Date   Day & Date

Coach's focus this week is: _____

_____

_____

My focus this week is: _____

_____

_____

How I feel looking ahead: _____

_____

_____

What I think I can contribute to the team this week: _____

_____

_____

My notes about this week's practice: _____

_____

_____

_____

_____

_____

_____

_____

Game Day

Game Date: _____ Game Time: _____

We played against: _____ Home ☐ Away ☐

Positions I played: _____ Final Score: _____

My summary: _____

_____

_____

_____

Coach's comments: _____

_____

_____

My contributions: _____

_____

_____

_____

Where I could have done better: _____

_____

_____

_____

Highlights of the game: _____

_____

_____

_____

_____

_____

Practice

Starting _____ until our next game on _____

Day & Date   Day & Date

Coach's focus this week is: _____

_____

_____

My focus this week is: _____

_____

_____

How I feel looking ahead: _____

_____

_____

What I think I can contribute to the team this week: _____

_____

_____

My notes about this week's practice: _____

_____

_____

_____

_____

_____

_____

_____

_____

Game Day

Game Date: _____ Game Time: _____

We played against: _____ Home ☐   Away ☐

Positions I played: _____ Final Score: _____

My summary: _____

_____

_____

_____

Coach's comments: _____

_____

_____

My contributions: _____

_____

_____

_____

Where I could have done better: _____

_____

_____

_____

Highlights of the game: _____

_____

_____

_____

_____

_____

Practice

Starting _____ until our next game on _____
                                             Day & Date

Coach's focus this week is: _____

_____

_____

My focus this week is: _____

_____

_____

How I feel looking ahead: _____

_____

_____

What I think I can contribute to the team this week: _____

_____

_____

My notes about this week's practice: _____

_____

_____

_____

_____

_____

_____

_____

Game Day

Game Date: _____ Game Time: _____

We played against: _____ Home ☐ Away ☐

Positions I played: _____ Final Score: _____

My summary: _____

_____

_____

_____

Coach's comments: _____

_____

_____

My contributions: _____

_____

_____

_____

Where I could have done better: _____

_____

_____

_____

Highlights of the game: _____

_____

_____

_____

_____

_____

Practice

Starting _____ until our next game on _____

Day & Date   Day & Date

Coach's focus this week is: _____

_____

_____

My focus this week is: _____

_____

_____

How I feel looking ahead: _____

_____

_____

What I think I can contribute to the team this week: _____

_____

_____

My notes about this week's practice: _____

_____

_____

_____

_____

_____

_____

_____

_____

Game Day

Game Date: _____ Game Time: _____

We played against: _____ Home ☐   Away ☐

Positions I played: _____ Final Score: _____

My summary: _____

_____

_____

_____

Coach's comments: _____

_____

_____

My contributions: _____

_____

_____

Where I could have done better: _____

_____

_____

Highlights of the game: _____

_____

_____

_____

_____

_____

Practice

Starting _____ until our next game on _____

Day & Date   Day & Date

Coach's focus this week is: _____

_____

_____

My focus this week is: _____

_____

_____

How I feel looking ahead: _____

_____

_____

What I think I can contribute to the team this week: _____

_____

_____

My notes about this week's practice: _____

_____

_____

_____

_____

_____

_____

_____

_____

Game Day

Game Date: _____ Game Time: _____

We played against: _____ Home ☐   Away ☐

Positions I played: _____ Final Score: _____

My summary: _____

_____

_____

_____

Coach's comments: _____

_____

_____

My contributions: _____

_____

_____

Where I could have done better: _____

_____

_____

_____

Highlights of the game: _____

_____

_____

_____

_____

_____

Practice

Starting _____ until our next game on _____
Day & Date   Day & Date

Coach's focus this week is: _____

_____

_____

My focus this week is: _____

_____

_____

How I feel looking ahead: _____

_____

_____

What I think I can contribute to the team this week: _____

_____

_____

My notes about this week's practice: _____

_____

_____

_____

_____

_____

_____

_____

Game Day

Game Date: _____ Game Time: _____

We played against: _____ Home ☐ Away ☐

Positions I played: _____ Final Score: _____

My summary: _____

_____

_____

_____

Coach's comments: _____

_____

_____

My contributions: _____

_____

_____

_____

Where I could have done better: _____

_____

_____

_____

Highlights of the game: _____

_____

_____

_____

_____

_____

_____

Practice

Starting _____ until our next game on _____
Day & Date   Day & Date

Coach's focus this week is: _____

_____

_____

My focus this week is: _____

_____

_____

How I feel looking ahead: _____

_____

_____

What I think I can contribute to the team this week: _____

_____

_____

My notes about this week's practice: _____

_____

_____

_____

_____

_____

_____

_____

Game Day

Game Date: _____ Game Time: _____

We played against: _____ Home ☐ Away ☐

Positions I played: _____ Final Score: _____

My summary: _____

_____

_____

_____

Coach's comments: _____

_____

_____

My contributions: _____

_____

_____

_____

Where I could have done better: _____

_____

_____

_____

Highlights of the game: _____

_____

_____

_____

_____

_____

Practice

Starting _____ until our next game on _____
         Day & Date   Day & Date

Coach's focus this week is: _____

_____

_____

My focus this week is: _____

_____

_____

How I feel looking ahead: _____

_____

_____

What I think I can contribute to the team this week: _____

_____

_____

My notes about this week's practice: _____

_____

_____

_____

_____

_____

_____

_____

Game Day

Game Date: _____ Game Time: _____

We played against: _____ Home ☐ Away ☐

Positions I played: _____ Final Score: _____

My summary: _____

_____

_____

_____

Coach's comments: _____

_____

_____

My contributions: _____

_____

_____

_____

Where I could have done better: _____

_____

_____

_____

Highlights of the game: _____

_____

_____

_____

_____

_____

Practice

Starting _____ until our next game on _____
Day & Date   Day & Date

Coach's focus this week is: _____

_____

My focus this week is: _____

_____

How I feel looking ahead: _____

_____

What I think I can contribute to the team this week: _____

_____

My notes about this week's practice: _____

_____

_____

_____

_____

_____

_____

_____

Game Day

Game Date: _____   Game Time: _____

We played against: _____   Home ☐   Away ☐

Positions I played: _____Final Score: _____

My summary: _____

_____

_____

_____

Coach's comments: _____

_____

_____

My contributions: _____

_____

_____

_____

Where I could have done better: _____

_____

_____

_____

Highlights of the game: _____

_____

_____

_____

_____

_____

Practice

Starting _____ until our next game on _____
Day & Date   Day & Date

Coach's focus this week is: _____
_____
_____

My focus this week is: _____
_____
_____

How I feel looking ahead: _____
_____
_____

What I think I can contribute to the team this week: _____
_____
_____

My notes about this week's practice: _____
_____
_____
_____
_____
_____
_____
_____

Game Day

Game Date: _____ Game Time: _____

We played against: _____ Home ☐   Away ☐

Positions I played: _____ Final Score: _____

My summary: _____

_____

_____

_____

Coach's comments: _____

_____

My contributions: _____

_____

_____

Where I could have done better: _____

_____

_____

Highlights of the game: _____

_____

_____

_____

_____

_____

Practice

Starting _____ until our next game on _____
Day & Date   Day & Date

Coach's focus this week is: _____

_____

_____

My focus this week is: _____

_____

_____

How I feel looking ahead: _____

_____

_____

What I think I can contribute to the team this week: _____

_____

_____

My notes about this week's practice: _____

_____

_____

_____

_____

_____

_____

_____

_____

Game Day

Game Date: _____ Game Time: _____

We played against: _____ Home ☐ Away ☐

Positions I played: _____ Final Score: _____

My summary: _____

_____

_____

_____

Coach's comments: _____

_____

_____

My contributions: _____

_____

_____

_____

Where I could have done better: _____

_____

_____

_____

Highlights of the game: _____

_____

_____

_____

_____

_____

Practice

Starting _____ until our next game on _____
          Day & Date   Day & Date

Coach's focus this week is: _____

_____

_____

My focus this week is: _____

_____

_____

How I feel looking ahead: _____

_____

_____

What I think I can contribute to the team this week: _____

_____

_____

My notes about this week's practice: _____

_____

_____

_____

_____

_____

_____

_____

_____

Game Day

Game Date: _____ Game Time: _____

We played against: _____ Home ☐ Away ☐

Positions I played: _____ Final Score: _____

My summary: _____

_____

_____

_____

Coach's comments: _____

_____

_____

My contributions: _____

_____

_____

_____

Where I could have done better: _____

_____

_____

_____

Highlights of the game: _____

_____

_____

_____

_____

_____

_____

Practice

Starting _____ until our next game on _____

Coach's focus this week is: _____

_____

_____

My focus this week is: _____

_____

_____

How I feel looking ahead: _____

_____

_____

What I think I can contribute to the team this week: _____

_____

_____

My notes about this week's practice: _____

_____

_____

_____

_____

_____

_____

_____

_____

Game Day

Game Date: _____ Game Time: _____

We played against: _____ Home ☐   Away ☐

Positions I played: _____ Final Score: _____

My summary: _____

_____

_____

_____

Coach's comments: _____

_____

_____

My contributions: _____

_____

_____

_____

Where I could have done better: _____

_____

_____

_____

Highlights of the game: _____

_____

_____

_____

_____

Practice

Starting _____ until our next game on _____
        <small>Day & Date</small>   <small>Day & Date</small>

Coach's focus this week is: _____

_____

_____

My focus this week is: _____

_____

_____

How I feel looking ahead: _____

_____

_____

What I think I can contribute to the team this week: _____

_____

_____

My notes about this week's practice: _____

_____

_____

_____

_____

_____

_____

_____

_____

Game Day

Game Date: _____   Game Time: _____

We played against: _____ Home ☐   Away ☐

Positions I played: _____ Final Score: _____

My summary: _____

_____

_____

_____

Coach's comments: _____

_____

_____

My contributions: _____

_____

_____

_____

Where I could have done better: _____

_____

_____

_____

Highlights of the game: _____

_____

_____

_____

_____

_____

_____

Practice

Starting _____ until our next game on _____
Day & Date Day & Date

Coach's focus this week is: _____

_____

_____

My focus this week is: _____

_____

_____

How I feel looking ahead: _____

_____

_____

What I think I can contribute to the team this week: _____

_____

_____

My notes about this week's practice: _____

_____

_____

_____

_____

_____

_____

_____

Game Day

Game Date: _____ Game Time: _____

We played against: _____ Home ☐   Away ☐

Positions I played: _____ Final Score: _____

My summary: _____

_____

_____

_____

Coach's comments: _____

_____

_____

My contributions: _____

_____

_____

_____

Where I could have done better: _____

_____

_____

_____

Highlights of the game: _____

_____

_____

_____

_____

_____

Practice

Starting _____ until our next game on _____

Day & Date   Day & Date

Coach's focus this week is: _____
_____
_____

My focus this week is: _____
_____
_____

How I feel looking ahead: _____
_____
_____

What I think I can contribute to the team this week: _____
_____
_____

My notes about this week's practice: _____
_____
_____
_____
_____
_____
_____
_____
_____

Game Day

Game Date: _____ Game Time: _____

We played against: _____ Home ☐ Away ☐

Positions I played: _____ Final Score: _____

My summary: _____

_____

_____

_____

Coach's comments: _____

_____

_____

My contributions: _____

_____

_____

_____

Where I could have done better: _____

_____

_____

_____

Highlights of the game: _____

_____

_____

_____

_____

_____

_____

Practice

Starting _____ until our next game on _____

Day & Date .... Day & Date

Coach's focus this week is: _____

_____

_____

My focus this week is: _____

_____

_____

How I feel looking ahead: _____

_____

_____

What I think I can contribute to the team this week: _____

_____

_____

My notes about this week's practice: _____

_____

_____

_____

_____

_____

_____

_____

Game Day

Game Date: _____ Game Time: _____

We played against: _____ Home ☐   Away ☐

Positions I played: _____ Final Score: _____

My summary: _____

_____

_____

_____

Coach's comments: _____

_____

_____

My contributions: _____

_____

_____

_____

Where I could have done better: _____

_____

_____

_____

Highlights of the game: _____

_____

_____

_____

_____

_____

Practice

Starting _____ until our next game on _____
Day & Date   Day & Date

Coach's focus this week is: _____

_____

My focus this week is: _____

_____

How I feel looking ahead: _____

_____

What I think I can contribute to the team this week: _____

_____

My notes about this week's practice: _____

_____

_____

_____

_____

_____

_____

_____

Game Day

Game Date: _____ Game Time: _____

We played against: _____ Home ☐ Away ☐

Positions I played: _____ Final Score: _____

My summary: _____

_____

_____

_____

Coach's comments: _____

_____

_____

My contributions: _____

_____

_____

_____

Where I could have done better: _____

_____

_____

_____

Highlights of the game: _____

_____

_____

_____

_____

_____

Practice

Starting _____ until our next game on _____

Coach's focus this week is: _____

_____

_____

My focus this week is: _____

_____

_____

How I feel looking ahead: _____

_____

_____

What I think I can contribute to the team this week: _____

_____

_____

My notes about this week's practice: _____

_____

_____

_____

_____

_____

_____

_____

Game Day

Game Date: _____ Game Time: _____

We played against: _____ Home ☐   Away ☐

Positions I played: _____Final Score: _____

My summary: _____

_____

_____

_____

Coach's comments: _____

_____

_____

My contributions: _____

_____

_____

Where I could have done better: _____

_____

_____

_____

Highlights of the game: _____

_____

_____

_____

_____

_____

Practice

Starting _____ until our next game on _____

Day & Date   Day & Date

Coach's focus this week is: _____

_____

_____

My focus this week is: _____

_____

_____

How I feel looking ahead: _____

_____

_____

What I think I can contribute to the team this week: _____

_____

_____

My notes about this week's practice: _____

_____

_____

_____

_____

_____

_____

_____

_____

Game Day

Game Date: _____ Game Time: _____

We played against: _____ Home ☐ Away ☐

Positions I played: _____Final Score: _____

My summary: _____

_____

_____

_____

Coach's comments: _____

_____

_____

My contributions: _____

_____

_____

_____

Where I could have done better: _____

_____

_____

Highlights of the game: _____

_____

_____

_____

_____

_____

Practice

Starting _____ until our next game on _____

Coach's focus this week is: _____

_____

_____

My focus this week is: _____

_____

_____

How I feel looking ahead: _____

_____

_____

What I think I can contribute to the team this week: _____

_____

_____

My notes about this week's practice: _____

_____

_____

_____

_____

_____

_____

_____

Game Day

Game Date: _____ Game Time: _____

We played against: _____ Home ☐   Away ☐

Positions I played: _____ Final Score: _____

My summary: _____

_____

_____

_____

Coach's comments: _____

_____

_____

My contributions: _____

_____

_____

_____

Where I could have done better: _____

_____

_____

_____

Highlights of the game: _____

_____

_____

_____

_____

_____

Practice

Starting _____ until our next game on _____
<small>Day & Date</small>   <small>Day & Date</small>

Coach's focus this week is: _____

_____

_____

My focus this week is: _____

_____

_____

How I feel looking ahead: _____

_____

_____

What I think I can contribute to the team this week: _____

_____

_____

My notes about this week's practice: _____

_____

_____

_____

_____

_____

_____

_____

Game Day

Game Date: _____ Game Time: _____

We played against: _____ Home ☐   Away ☐

Positions I played: _____Final Score: _____

My summary: _____

_____

_____

_____

Coach's comments: _____

_____

_____

My contributions: _____

_____

_____

_____

Where I could have done better: _____

_____

_____

_____

Highlights of the game: _____

_____

_____

_____

_____

_____

Practice

Starting _____ until our next game on _____

Coach's focus this week is: _____

_____

_____

My focus this week is: _____

_____

_____

How I feel looking ahead: _____

_____

_____

What I think I can contribute to the team this week: _____

_____

_____

My notes about this week's practice: _____

_____

_____

_____

_____

_____

_____

_____

_____

_____

Game Day

Game Date: _____ Game Time: _____

We played against: _____ Home ☐ Away ☐

Positions I played: _____ Final Score: _____

My summary: _____

_____

_____

_____

Coach's comments: _____

_____

_____

My contributions: _____

_____

_____

Where I could have done better: _____

_____

_____

_____

Highlights of the game: _____

_____

_____

_____

_____

_____

Practice

Starting _____ until our next game on _____
Day & Date   Day & Date

Coach's focus this week is: _____

_____

_____

My focus this week is: _____

_____

_____

How I feel looking ahead: _____

_____

_____

What I think I can contribute to the team this week: _____

_____

_____

My notes about this week's practice: _____

_____

_____

_____

_____

_____

_____

_____

_____

Game Day

Game Date: _____   Game Time: _____

We played against: _____   Home ☐   Away ☐

Positions I played: _____Final Score: _____

My summary: _____

_____

_____

_____

Coach's comments: _____

_____

_____

My contributions: _____

_____

_____

_____

Where I could have done better: _____

_____

_____

_____

Highlights of the game: _____

_____

_____

_____

_____

_____

Practice

Starting _____ until our next game on _____
Day & Date   Day & Date

Coach's focus this week is: _____

_____

_____

My focus this week is: _____

_____

_____

How I feel looking ahead: _____

_____

_____

What I think I can contribute to the team this week: _____

_____

_____

My notes about this week's practice: _____

_____

_____

_____

_____

_____

_____

_____

Game Day

Game Date: _____ Game Time: _____

We played against: _____ Home ☐   Away ☐

Positions I played: _____ Final Score: _____

My summary: _____

_____

_____

_____

Coach's comments: _____

_____

_____

My contributions: _____

_____

_____

_____

Where I could have done better: _____

_____

_____

_____

Highlights of the game: _____

_____

_____

_____

_____

_____

Practice

Starting _____ until our next game on _____
Day & Date   Day & Date

Coach's focus this week is: _____

_____

_____

My focus this week is: _____

_____

_____

How I feel looking ahead: _____

_____

_____

What I think I can contribute to the team this week: _____

_____

_____

My notes about this week's practice: _____

_____

_____

_____

_____

_____

_____

_____

_____

Game Day

Game Date: _____ Game Time: _____

We played against: _____ Home ☐   Away ☐

Positions I played: _____Final Score: _____

My summary: _____

_____

_____

_____

Coach's comments: _____

_____

_____

My contributions: _____

_____

_____

_____

Where I could have done better: _____

_____

_____

_____

Highlights of the game: _____

_____

_____

_____

_____

_____

_____

Practice

Starting _____ until our next game on _____
Day & Date   Day & Date

Coach's focus this week is: _____

_____

_____

My focus this week is: _____

_____

_____

How I feel looking ahead: _____

_____

_____

What I think I can contribute to the team this week: _____

_____

_____

My notes about this week's practice: _____

_____

_____

_____

_____

_____

_____

_____

Game Day

Game Date: _____ Game Time: _____

We played against: _____ Home ☐   Away ☐

Positions I played: _____Final Score: _____

My summary: _____

_____

_____

_____

Coach's comments: _____

_____

_____

My contributions: _____

_____

_____

_____

Where I could have done better: _____

_____

_____

_____

Highlights of the game: _____

_____

_____

_____

_____

_____

_____

Practice

Starting _____ until our next game on _____
Day & Date   Day & Date

Coach's focus this week is: _____

_____

_____

My focus this week is: _____

_____

_____

How I feel looking ahead: _____

_____

_____

What I think I can contribute to the team this week: _____

_____

_____

My notes about this week's practice: _____

_____

_____

_____

_____

_____

_____

_____

_____

Game Day

Game Date: _____ Game Time: _____

We played against: _____ Home ☐   Away ☐

Positions I played: _____ Final Score: _____

My summary: _____

_____

_____

_____

Coach's comments: _____

_____

_____

My contributions: _____

_____

_____

_____

Where I could have done better: _____

_____

_____

_____

Highlights of the game: _____

_____

_____

_____

_____

_____

Practice

Starting _____ until our next game on _____
Day & Date   Day & Date

Coach's focus this week is: _____

_____

_____

My focus this week is: _____

_____

_____

How I feel looking ahead: _____

_____

_____

What I think I can contribute to the team this week: _____

_____

_____

My notes about this week's practice: _____

_____

_____

_____

_____

_____

_____

_____

What a season you've had!
You've used up 29 of your
worksheet sets.
There's one more after this page.
Use it to make as many
photocopies as you need
to complete your season.

Game Day

Game Date: _____ Game Time: _____

We played against: _____ Home ☐ Away ☐

Positions I played: _____ Final Score: _____

My summary: _____

_____

_____

_____

Coach's comments: _____

_____

_____

My contributions: _____

_____

_____

_____

Where I could have done better: _____

_____

_____

_____

Highlights of the game: _____

_____

_____

_____

_____

_____

_____

Practice

Starting _____ until our next game on _____
Day & Date   Day & Date

Coach's focus this week is: _____

_____

_____

My focus this week is: _____

_____

_____

How I feel looking ahead: _____

_____

_____

What I think I can contribute to the team this week: _____

_____

_____

My notes about this week's practice: _____

_____

_____

_____

_____

_____

_____

_____

My
BASEBALL
Season
Memories

Memories

Memories

Memories

Memories

About the Author

Karleen Tauszik writes books mostly for children ages 8 to 12. Her goal as an author is to get kids to LOVE reading. She is married to a professional ventriloquist and magician, and they live in the Tampa Bay area. Learn more about Karleen and her other books at her website, KarleenT.com. Ask a parent to sign up for her newsletter so you'll be the first to know about new books.

Interested in other sports? Look for the rest of the "My Season" Journals:

My Softball Season

My Soccer Season

My Hockey Season

My Basketball Season

My Football Season

Made in the USA
Monee, IL
26 March 2022

93601473R00046